SCIENCE ON PATROL

in the Desert

**Louise and
Richard Spilsbury**

Gareth Stevens
PUBLISHING

Please visit our website, www.garethstevens.com.
For a free color catalog of all our high-quality books,
call toll free 1-800-542-2595 or fax 1-877-542-2596.

Cataloging-in-Publication Data

Names: Spilsbury, Louise.
Title: In the desert / Louise and Richard Spilsbury.
Description: New York : Gareth Stevens, 2017. | Series: Science on patrol | Includes index.
Identifiers: ISBN 9781482459760 (pbk.) | ISBN 9781482459784 (library bound) | ISBN 9781482459777 (6 pack)
Subjects: LCSH: Deserts--Juvenile literature.
Classification: LCC QH88.S65 2017 | DDC 577.54--dc23

First Edition

Published in 2017 by
Gareth Stevens Publishing
111 East 14th Street, Suite 349
New York, NY 10003

Copyright © 2017 Gareth Stevens Publishing

Produced for Gareth Stevens by Calcium
Editors: Sarah Eason and Jennifer Sanderson
Designers: Paul Myerscough and Simon Borrough
Picture researcher: Rachel Blount

Picture credits: Cover: Shutterstock: AP Design (top), ESO (b); Inside: Desert Research Institute: George Nikolich 19; NASA: David Wettergreen/Carnegie Mellon University 37; Shutterstock: Algol 45t, Marianne Campolongo 18, Rusty Dodson 8–9t, Cat Downie 11, ChameleonsEye 43, EcoPrint 8, Michael Egenburg 12, EpicStockMedia 3, 14, GeNik 36, JeniFoto 5, Matt Jeppson 32, LobsteR 27, Clari Massimiliano 39, Cleverson Ivan Merlo 10, Mezzotint 26, OfffStock 1, 44–45, Pavelk 41, Ruth Peterkin 29b, Maxim Petrichuk 7, Protasov AN 28–29, Sergei25 13, Nickolay Stanev 40, Beth Swanson 17, G Tipene 16, Vixit 6–7, Dan Vojtech photographer 38, Waj 35, Yarygin 30–31, Piotr Zajda 34, Oleg Znamenskiy 4; Wikimedia Commons: Matt Lavin from Bozeman, Montana, USA 15, Dr Jake Maule/NASA 25, 42, Hugh McGregor 33, NASA 24, David Shankbone 21, Wilson44691 22–23.

Printed in China
CPSIA compliance information: Batch #CW17GS: For further information contact Gareth Stevens, New York, New York at 1-800-542-2595.

contents

Chapter 1 Working in the Desert 4
Challenges and Changes 6
Daily Dangers...................................8

Chapter 2 Why Study Deserts?.....................10
Desertification 12
Habitat Destruction 14
Desert Dust 16

Chapter 3 Lab Life 18
Off-Grid 20
Lab Tour 22
Space in the Desert...........................24

Chapter 4 Out and About 26
Survival Gear 28
Be Prepared 30

Chapter 5 Cutting-Edge Technology 32
Studying Sun and Rain 34
Desert Robots...................................36
Mapping Sand and Water.....................38

Chapter 6 Amazing Discoveries 40
Using Desert Discoveries......................42
Patrolling the Future...........................44

Glossary 46
For More Information 47
Index 48

working in the desert

The hot deserts of the world are a challenging and sometimes dangerous place to work. Scientists on patrol in these sandy, rocky wildernesses may have to cope with burning hot days, freezing nights, a lack of water, and windblown sand blasting them for hours on end.

The desert is a challenging habitat in which to live and work.

Desert Environments

Many people think of deserts as huge expanses of flat sand. However, deserts are far more varied than you might imagine. Some deserts are rugged and mountainous. In others, sand dunes rise above the surface like large hills and shift with the wind. A desert is defined as a place that gets less than 10 inches (254 millimeters) of rain per year. With such little water, fewer plants and animals can survive in deserts than elsewhere. However, deserts are still rich **habitats** for many living things. In some deserts, tall palm trees and grasses grow around oases. These pools of water in the desert spring up from deep under the ground.

How Deserts Form

• **Subtropical deserts:** Air above the **equator** is very hot and moist, and drops heavy rains. This makes air moving toward the **tropics** cooler and drier. Subtropical deserts include the Sahara and Kalahari in Africa and the Tanami in Australia.

• **Coastal deserts:** When air blows over a coast from a cold ocean, it is cool enough to form fog but not fall as rain. This creates coastal deserts such as the Atacama on the Pacific coast of Chile. The Atacama Desert is the driest place on Earth.

• **Rain shadow deserts:** When moist air rises up a mountain range, its moisture **condenses** and falls as rain. When the air reaches the other side of the range, no more moisture is left, creating a desert. Death Valley in the United States is a desert in the shadow of the Sierra Nevada Mountains.

• **Inland deserts:** Some deserts form because they are so far inland that no winds carrying moisture from the oceans reach them. The Gobi, in China and Mongolia, is an inland desert.

Challenges and Changes

Scientists who study deserts have bases and labs to live and work in, but they also need to venture out on patrol. When they travel out into a desert to collect **samples** and **data**, they face the challenges of the desert **climate**.

The Sahara is the largest desert in the world and one of the hottest places on Earth.

Desert Heat

Some deserts are so hot during the day that any rain that falls quickly **evaporates** and disappears. Daytime temperatures in the Sahara, for example, are often as high as 122° Fahrenheit (50° Celsius). Dry desert heat can be exhausting and dangerous. There are few trees or rocks to provide shade, so it is easy to overheat. If people get too hot for too long, they can get heatstroke. Heatstroke is a serious condition that happens when the body loses its ability to cool down. People become so hot they stop sweating and can collapse and lose consciousness. If untreated, heatstroke can damage the brain and other internal organs.

Sudden Rain

Overall, there is very little rainfall in deserts. Some deserts may go without any rain for several years at a time. Coastal deserts get a little **precipitation**, but it comes from condensed fog, not rain. Any rain that does fall in the desert usually falls over limited periods, usually for around 15 to 20 days a year.

When rain falls in these short periods, it can be very heavy. It can cause floods that suddenly wash across the land because the water cannot soak into the hard ground quickly enough.

Sandstorms

Another challenge facing scientists in the desert is the risk of sandstorms. When winds blow across a desert surface, they pick up sand and blow it against things. A sandstorm can start suddenly and close in quickly. Sandstorms can fill the sky and make it hard for people to breathe or to see where they are going.

The wind whips up a sandstorm in the Altyn-Emel National Park desert in Kazakhstan.

Daily Dangers

When scientists work outdoors in deserts, they face other dangers in addition to the heat. There are animals that can deliver painful or fatal stings, and there are areas of the desert where it is unsafe to walk.

Animal Dangers

Deserts may look empty, but there are many animals hiding from the sun under the sand and behind rocks. Many desert animals are harmless. There are small rodents that feed on plants and seeds, for example. But some desert animals are more dangerous. Scorpions have a large, curved tail that can curl forward to inject **venom** into victims through a stinger at its end. Scorpions often hurt people who step on them by mistake or who pull on shoes when a scorpion has crawled inside them.

When scorpions need to attack, they curl their stinger forward.

A bite from a
Gila monster is
incredibly painful,
but it is unlikely
to result in death.

Rattlesnakes and Gila Monsters

Rattlesnakes are not aggressive and do not usually attack humans. If they are stepped on or feel cornered, however, they can deliver a potentially deadly bite. Rattlesnakes inject venom into a victim using sharp, hollow fangs (teeth) that are like curved **hypodermic needles**. The fangs fold back when not in use, but unfold to attack. Rattlesnake venom can kill. Gila monsters are poisonous lizards. They also tend to avoid humans, but will bite if they feel threatened. Unlike rattlesnakes, gila monsters chew their venom into a victim's skin rather than injecting it through fangs.

SCIENCE PATROL SURVIVAL

Quicksand is a serious danger for scientists in the desert. Quicksand is a patch of sand that contains so much water it loses its ability to support any weight, and becomes more like a liquid. Quicksand occurs when water flowing underground soaks an area of loose sand above it. If someone accidentally sinks in a patch of quicksand and panics and struggles, the sand can suck them under and they can drown.

How do you think dealing with these daily challenges might affect scientists as they work? Give reasons for your answers.

why study deserts?

Scientists study deserts to learn about their distinctive plants and animals, and the **adaptations** that allow them to live in the **arid** environment. Scientists also try to figure out why and how deserts are spreading in some areas, and how human actions threaten desert habitats.

Plant Adaptations

In some deserts, plants have to go a whole year without a single drop of rain. Scientists are discovering all kinds of adaptations used by desert shrubs, flowers, and other plants to survive the heat, **drought**, and poor soil in the desert. Cactus plants have stems that can swell to store water for times of drought. They have shallow root systems that spread out widely in order to collect as much water as possible. In contrast, the velvet mesquite shrub in the Sonoran Desert gets the water it needs through roots that grow 165 feet (50 meters) down into the ground.

The spines on a cactus protect the plant from animals trying to get to the water in its stems.

Animal Adaptations

Many desert animals are **nocturnal**. They come out only at night, when it is cooler, and spend the day in caves or in burrows under the ground, out of the sun. The desert tortoise spends most of its time underground. Desert birds, such as the roadrunner, survive on very little water because they get liquid from the animals they eat. Scorpions have a thick exoskeleton (outer covering) that reduces the amount of water they lose through their skin.

New Species

Desert scientists regularly discover new species, or types, of animals and plants. For example, in 2014, in the desert of Morocco, scientists found a new spider: the flic-flac spider. During the day, this spider hides underground in a tubelike structure with a sandy lid. It comes out at night to look for food. It is named for the amazing way it can move to escape **predators**. It moves by means of "flic-flac" jumps. Like an acrobat, it runs to gather speed, then jumps off the ground and performs a series of rapid flic-flac rolls that allow it to move twice as fast as it normally does.

The fennec fox has huge ears to help it lose body heat and keep cool. →

11

Desertification

Scientists are researching how the area of Earth's surface covered in deserts is increasing, especially in **semidesert** regions. The change is not caused by drought or a lack of water but by human actions, such as overgrazing of livestock. This process is known as desertification.

Overgrazing

Overgrazing is an issue on the fringes of many of the world's large deserts. Overgrazing occurs when too many cattle, goats, or sheep are allowed to feed on an area of land with sparse vegetation. They eat all of the plants, leaving only bare soil. The animals' hooves pound the land and further damage the soil. When this happens, the dry land becomes dusty. The top layer of soil, which is rich in the **nutrients** that new plants need to grow, washes away in the rain or blows away in the wind. This leaves soil that is **infertile**.

Overgrazing by millions of sheep, cattle, and goats is the main cause of degraded land and desertification in many parts of the world.

Slow Recovery

It can take many years for soil to recover after it has been overgrazed. Some land never recovers. Instead, it gradually turns into desert. Without plants to eat, livestock dies. Without farm animals to supply them with food, many of the people who live in or near deserts face hunger or starvation.

Global Warming

Global warming may also cause desertification. The term describes the gradual increase in the average temperature of Earth's **atmosphere**. Global warming is increasing the number of droughts around the world and making them last longer. This makes land drier and subject to **erosion**, and it dries up oases and water holes. More heat means that more water evaporates into the air, taking moisture from already-dry soils.

Plants normally hold moisture, which evaporates into the air and can form clouds and rain. When there are no more plants, the soil and air become drier and the land becomes parched.

Habitat Destruction

Understanding how human activities impact desert regions is vital to understanding how to protect the wildlife and people there. Scientists are studying the ways in which activities, such as mining and tourism, and the introduction of new species of plants, affect deserts.

Industrial Impacts

Some deserts hold massive stores of oil below their surface. More than half of the oil reserves in the world lie beneath the Arabian Desert, mostly in Saudi Arabia. Some scientists work in deserts to locate sources of oil. Others study the impacts of oil mining and how to lessen the disruption that oil and gas production can cause to sensitive desert habitats. There are also minerals, such as gold, beneath desert lands. People build mines to extract the minerals. The mines may use water to extract or clean the minerals, removing precious **groundwater** from the desert. They may also use chemicals that affect the desert. For example, potassium cyanide can be used to separate gold and silver **particles** from **ore**. When potassium cyanide leaks into groundwater, it can poison wildlife.

Some scientists help companies decide where to drill for oil in desert regions.

Tourism Troubles

When tourists visit deserts, they often travel using off-road vehicles, such as dirt bikes, all-terrain vehicles, and jeeps. When these vehicles are used irresponsibly, they can destroy plants that desert animals need to eat, crush burrows, and compact soil, making it harder for plants to grow. Scientists are studying what damage tourism causes desert habitats and how this impacts specific animals, such as the desert tortoise.

Alien Invaders

Plant invaders are plants from one region of the world that start to grow and spread in a new part of the world. They can cause problems when they take over from native plants. For example, a Mediterranean plant called red brome grass is spreading quickly in some U.S. deserts. The seeds are widely distributed in the wind, and they need about half as much water as most native plant seeds to **germinate**. The problem is that red brome grass has sharp, pointed florets that can irritate livestock. The plants also burn easily. This increases the number of fires in desert regions, killing native plants on which many desert **food chains** rely.

Red brome grass seeds were probably brought to the United States accidentally in the nineteenth century. The plants have since spread across the country.

15

Desert Dust

Scientists study how, where, and when desert dust forms, where it travels to, and how it affects land and oceans far away.

In 2009, Sydney, Australia, was covered in red dust blown in from the **outback**.

Dust on the Move

Deserts create a lot of dust, which the wind can blow to nondesert areas. Scientists have observed that tiny desert dust particles are usually released into the air when slightly larger particles are blown by the wind and bounce off the desert soil. Dust comes from many deserts, but most of the dust in Earth's atmosphere comes from the very dry deserts in northern Africa and Asia. Small dust particles can be carried thousands of miles by strong winds.

Dust Effects

Wind-blown desert dust can have positive and negative effects. The dust contains minerals, such as phosphorus and silicon, which can add nutrients to ecosystems on land and in the oceans. For example, desert dust that falls in oceans can help **phytoplankton** grow. Phytoplankton are a vital first link in many ocean food chains. Tons of dust also blow from the Sahara onto the Amazon rainforest every year. In the Amazon, soils are poor because heavy rains wash nutrients out of the soil. The desert dust adds nutrients to the soil that help rainforest plants grow.

On the downside, desert dust in the air can reduce visibility for cars and planes, and may cause accidents. Dust storms also cause breathing problems and diseases. Some scientists are investigating whether increased amounts of dust in the Atlantic carried the **bacteria** that have contributed to the destruction of **coral reefs** there.

Is there a link between desert dust and the death of coral reefs?

SCIENCE PATROL SURVIVAL

Some scientists are researching the effects of global warming on desert dust. In deserts that become drier and windier, there is likely to be more dust. In deserts that are predicted to get more rain, desert dust may be reduced.

How do you think scientific discoveries about the effects of phenomena such as global warming and windblown dust can make a difference to how governments treat deserts and prepare for dust storms?

CHAPTER 3
LAB LiFe

Scientists who carry out research in deserts do a lot of their work in labs. They may go out into the field to collect data and carry out experiments, but they usually return to the labs to study further and make conclusions about their work to share with other scientists.

Types of Lab

Some desert research labs are large facilities or institutes with room for scientists and on-site support staff to live and work. The staff may maintain and operate machinery, including vehicles the scientists use to go out on patrol, and provide services such as meals for visiting scientists. Other labs are smaller with much less space. Scientists use them for very specialized areas of study. Here are a few examples of specialized labs:

Wildland Fire Science Center: Labs such as this one are for scientists who study wildfires. They study how plants and animals in deserts respond and adapt to fire, how fires and their effects may change in the future, and how firefighters can tackle desert blazes.

Fires can wipe out entire areas of desert plants like these.

The Storm Peak Laboratory: This lab is built at around 3,000 feet (1,150 meters) up a bare mountainside in Colorado. Scientists come here to measure gases and other chemicals in the atmosphere and how storms happen. This site has especially clear air, with less pollution than at lower levels.

PI-SWERL: PI-SWERL stands for Portable In-Situ Wind Erosion Lab. It is a moveable wind machine that blows desert sand and soil past monitors. These measure the dust thrown into the air. Using this lab is quicker and cheaper and takes fewer people than setting up a wind tunnel and separate monitors at a desert lab.

PI-SWERL has a cart that transports instruments and equipment.

Off-Grid

The different kinds of desert settings that scientists want to study are often off-grid. This means the labs scientists use there have no connection to power lines, water, and sewage pipes. It may also mean the labs are remote and are not accessible by roads.

Power Supply

The obvious source of energy in hot deserts is the sun. Many desert labs make electricity using **solar power** with photovoltaic (PV) panels. These panels are made from layers of materials that convert light energy to electrical energy. PV panels can be mounted on roofs or arranged on the ground. The panels do not work at night when it is dark, so power is stored during the daytime in large batteries. In less-sunny deserts, or at night, scientists may also rely on power produced by spinning **wind turbines** or even by burning fuel in generators.

Water Source

Some desert labs have natural water sources, such as springs or wells, with access to groundwater deep underground. The water is rarely safe to drink. Often it is too **contaminated** to be used in experiments because it contains dissolved minerals and bacteria. Some labs may use spring or well water for the scientists' showers or washing dishes. Desert labs may have special water-purifying machines to make the water safe enough to drink. In the driest desert locations, scientists may need to bring in all their water in containers when they arrive.

Walkways at a desert research lab may be shaded to keep scientists from getting too hot when moving between buildings.

SCIENCE PATROL SURVIVAL

Keeping cool in a desert lab is difficult. Labs cannot run air conditioners because they have limited power supplies. Some labs are designed to keep cool in the desert sun. They have windows positioned under shading roofs to keep light and heat from entering. Buildings may also use evaporative cooling. This means that hot air is allowed to evaporate to cool the building. For example, they may have roofs with an air gap underneath to allow hot air inside to escape. They may also have coolers that use the cooling effect caused by evaporating liquids.

Give examples of desert animals that use evaporative cooling. Research ways in which buildings are naturally cooled in hot climates.

Lab Tour

Each desert lab is different, depending on its size, location, and the scientific studies that happen there. The Desert Studies Center (DSC) in California is fairly typical.

The DSC is located within the Mojave Desert at an oasis called Zzyzx, or Soda Springs. It is a field station of the California State University, built on the site of an old mining settlement. In the past, people came here to mine borax, which is a mineral used in industry, for example, to make ovenproof glass. The DSC is made up of several buildings.

Living quarters: There is housing for up to 75 people in dormitory rooms. There are also two research residences that can house up to five scientists each. These are self-contained with a kitchen and bath.

Main hall: The main hall is usually set up as a dining room but it can be changed for meetings of up to 60 people. It has presentation equipment, such as chalkboards, flip charts, and overhead projectors, as well as computers and wifi.

Reference material: The small library in the DSC has many books, journals, maps, and university research papers that focus on the local area. In addition to the library, the DSC has a collection of living and dead **organisms** for scientists to study and compare their findings. These include a herbarium, in which local desert plants are growing.

The laboratory: This large space has a lot of work space, such as counter tops and equipment available for visiting scientists to use. There are refrigerators to store chemicals and **specimens**, ovens for drying soil samples, machines to crush rocks, and balances to weigh samples. Scientists have access to typical laboratory equipment, including Bunsen burners, glass jars, and measuring cylinders, and filters for separating solids from liquids. The DSC has optical equipment, too, from hand lenses and microscopes to astronomical telescopes for observing the stars.

You can see the large piles of rock surrounding the DSC, which miners left behind. They are next to an oasis of salty water. Can you see the DSC weather station?

SPACE IN THE DESERT

Some scientists use deserts as laboratories to help astronauts survive in and study space. Many deserts are similar to the moon or planets such as Mars, because they are remote, dusty, bare, rocky, and switch from baking hot by day to freezing cold at night.

Life on Mars

Mars is the only other planet in Earth's solar system where humans might be able to live. Even though they cannot fly there yet, NASA's Desert Research and Technology Studies (RATS) team is designing and developing technology, such as rover vehicles and living pods, which astronauts might use on Mars in future missions

Researchers test planetary exploration vehicles in desert conditions so they can make modifications to improve their performance. →

During the process of developing the LOCAD bacteria sensor, scientists in the desert use swabs to check for bacteria on a spacesuit.

Make-Believe

Scientists take part in mock Mars missions in which they can go outside wearing only space suits and live in pods or work in labs the rest of the time. Even though the air is safe to breathe in the desert, scientists use conditions to practice being on Mars, where there is not enough oxygen to survive. They can test things such as whether the suits are airtight or become too hot to wear, and how well communication systems work between spacesuit, pods, rovers, and Earth. Such testing could be critical in the future, not only to help prevent disasters but also to enable exciting space discoveries.

Space Technology on Earth

Scientific work on space missions has developed many useful things for people on Earth, such as Velcro and plastic windshields for jet airplanes. The RATS team tests innovations in desert labs for space exploration that might help on our planet, too. For example, they have made a special electronic sensor called LOCAD to rapidly test for bacteria on space suits. LOCAD could stop the accidental spread of Earth bacteria to other planets via space missions, but could also help protect our planet. Doctors may be able to use it to check the spread of dangerous bacterial diseases.

CHAPTER 4

OUT and About

The desert is a challenging place to travel, work, and stay in, so scientists need a range of equipment and vehicles to help them survive when they are out and about on patrol.

Navigation

Deserts can be difficult to **navigate** because they are so vast. Many expanses of sand look the same, so it is easy to become lost. Sand dunes can also shift in the wind, making it difficult to locate helpful landmarks. Scientists on patrol carry a compass, a map, and a **Global Positioning System (GPS)** device. A compass needle always points north, a map has features such as high hills marked to help navigate, and so with a map and a compass, people can figure out directions. GPS units use **satellite** links to pinpoint locations.

GPS units work well in the desert. The sky is clear, which helps the units communicate with satellites.

The tires on a 4x4 vehicle are designed to grip tricky terrain such as the sand and rocks on a desert trail.

Vehicles

In the past, the only way to travel long distances into the desert was by camel. Camels are still used in some deserts today, but most scientists use SUVs or four-wheel-drive vehicles. These tend to have high wheels that hold the body of the vehicle away from rocks that can damage the underside. They also have wide wheels for spreading the load and tires that are better at gripping loose surfaces, making it possible to climb hills of sand. Teams of scientists always check a vehicle carefully before setting out. They carry a full tool kit and spare tires. Scientists usually travel in groups for safety, in case a vehicle does break down.

Hazards

Desert travel is slow. One reason is that the land is rocky or sandy, which causes more **friction** than a smooth road and slows down tires. The other reason is that, by driving slowly, scientists are more likely to spot hazards, such as areas of quicksand that could swallow a vehicle or deep ruts in the road that could scrape a vehicle. Driving slowly also ensures people have time to avoid driving over plants or wildlife, so they do less damage to desert tracks and the desert environment.

SURVIVAL GEAR

Before scientists set out on patrol in the desert, they have to make sure they have the right equipment and supplies to survive the blazing heat. They need suitable clothing for protection against the weather extremes and a survival kit.

Clothes are usually made from fabrics that are thin and lightweight but also protect people from the sun. Light colors reflect the sun's rays, and dark colors absorb them.

Sun Care

There is no shade or cloud cover in the desert and the sun reflects off the sand, so it hits the skin twice. The sun's **ultraviolet (UV)** rays can cause severe sunburn, even when it does not seem very bright. Severe sunburn is not only painful. It can also make people sick and it can be fatal. Scientists tend to wear long, loose pants and shirts that cover the skin, but also allow air to circulate as this helps keep people cooler. People should wear sunblock on any parts of their skin not covered by clothes.

Sun Damage

The head, neck, and eyes are the areas most commonly affected by sun damage, so it is important to wear a hat with a wide brim that goes all the way round. Sunglasses protect the eyes, even on cloudy days, because UV rays still pass through clouds. Wearing sunglasses or goggles also helps protect the eyes from windblown dust and sand that can damage them or make them sore.

Winds can move quickly across deserts because there are few obstacles to block or slow their movement. They can also blow sand into the eyes.

Safety Supplies

In the desert, people are usually far away from the nearest hospital or town. Even a minor injury can become serious because it can take so long to call for help. That is why scientists take a first-aid kit with them. As well as medicines and bandages, the kit also includes an antivenom pump for scorpion stings and snakebites, and insect repellent to keep biting bugs at bay. It may also include a lip balm to keep the dry heat from causing cracking and bleeding in lips, eye drops to soothe eyes sore from dust, and salt tablets to replace salts lost through sweating.

BE PREPARED

Scientists on patrol may travel so far from their base station to collect samples and data that they have to stay in the desert overnight or longer. They have to set up a camp and take equipment to survive the cold at night.

A tent protects scientists from windblown dust and chilly temperatures in the desert at night.

Camping Out

It is so hot in deserts during the day because there are no clouds to filter the sun. The sunlight heats the ground, which heats the air. At night, that heat escapes because there are no clouds to trap it near the ground, so temperatures drop to just above freezing. It is vital to sleep in a vehicle or take shelter in a tent.

Taking Food Supplies

As deserts are so dry, there are very few plants to eat and fewer animals that eat plants. This means it is very hard to find anything to eat in the wild, so scientists need to take all their food supplies with them when they set out. They avoid taking food that melts or becomes rotten quickly in the heat. Scientists must take meals that are high in calories for their weight, such as energy bars.

Carrying Water

It is also vital for scientists to take water supplies. Every hour people spend in a very hot desert, they can lose about 1 pint (500 milliliters) of water in sweat, even when they are sitting still. If scientists do not replace the fluids that they lose through sweat, they are in danger of becoming **dehydrated** and this can be very dangerous.

SCIENCE PATROL SURVIVAL

When scientists work and camp in remote parts of the desert, they are careful to dispose of their waste properly. They pack up all trash, leftover food, and litter, and take it away with them. They dig deep holes for human waste and cover them when finished.

Why do you think taking measures such as disposing of waste carefully is very important?

CHAPTER 5

Cutting-Edge Technology

A lot of the technology scientists use to do their research in the field is familiar to everyone. For example, scientists may use long-handled grabbers and hooks to capture snakes and put them carefully into collecting bags. Some technology for studying animals, however, is more cutting edge.

Camera Traps

Smartphone species recognition can help keep an eye on the health of populations of animals such as desert tortoises.

To spot sandy colored animals against expanses of sand, scientists often use camera traps. These are digital cameras that take pictures when an animal walks through an infrared beam. Camera traps take images of anything that moves, so if a scientist is studying only one or two species he or she might have to go through hundreds of photos to identify the ones they need. This is boring and can take a very long time—time they could be using to do more important work. So, they invented a faster solution using smartphones.

Smartphone Software

Scientists have developed software that can identify particular animal species. The software scans the landscape for objects that could be animals. It searches for patterns of pixels (the dots that make up a digital image) that are new to the scene, and compares these patterns with a database of pixel patterns corresponding to individual animals. This means the software can tell the difference between a desert tortoise or squirrel and a rock or a tumbleweed, so it only takes images of the animals scientists are studying.

Tracking Movements

GPS collars can be used to track animals' movements across the desert. Animals might have GPS tags attached to them, for example, built into sturdy collars to put around the necks of camels or on delicate rings to put around birds' legs. Their movements are tracked on laptop computers and the animals' changing locations over time are recorded.

The wild brush-tailed rock-wallaby on the left is fitted with a radio tracking collar.

STUDYING SUN AND RAIN

Cutting-edge technology is at work in deserts, helping researchers harness the abundant sunlight in deserts and increase rainfall.

New Solar Power

Las Vegas in Nevada is a desert city of around 600,000 people. It gets 10 hours of all its daily electricity from solar power without using solar panels. The electricity comes from a concentrated solar power station made up of 10,347 billboard-sized mirrors called heliostats. Each heliostat reflects sunlight onto a 540-feet (165 meter) high central power tower. The concentrated light from all the heliostats warms the top of the power tower. Inside the power tower are pipes filled with molten (melted) salt that heats up even more. The super-hot salt is then used to boil water to make steam. The steam spins generators, creating electricity.

This steam-driven solar power plant is in the Nevada Desert.

Heat Store

Molten salt can store heat for years, so it can be used to generate power day and night, as long as it is supplied with more heat and prevented from cooling. However, it takes an enormous amount of energy to melt salt in the first place. Scientists have discovered a new heat store for electricity generation: sand. Sand can heat up to 1,832° Fahrenheit (1,000° Celsius)—and, of course, it is abundant in deserts.

Some scientists believe desert sand may be the answer to the problem of storing solar energy to make electricity at night when the sun does not shine.

Rain making

Cloud seeding is the process of creating clouds by putting very cold particles of chemicals in the sky. Water vapor in the atmosphere condenses and freezes onto the particles, forming clouds that can produce rain. Until recently, cloud seeding was done from airplanes or by firing rockets from the ground, but these techniques are expensive and hazardous. Now, scientists have developed flying robots, or drones, that can seed clouds over deserts without any danger to the pilot on the ground, even in adverse weather conditions.

Desert ROBOTS

Some of the most cutting-edge technology used for desert research is found in robots. Robots are machines that can carry out tasks automatically, based on computer programming. Using robots avoids the dangers of placing human researchers in remote deserts, and robots can collect data for weeks on end without needing food, water, or shelter.

Tumbleweed Robots

Tumbleweed is a North American desert plant with globe-shaped branches that break away from its roots. The wind blows the plant across the ground. The Tumbleweed robot uses a similar principle to move. When the wind blows, the robot opens up sails that form a sphere and allow it to catch the wind and roll. The robot cannot control where it goes as it blows with the wind. Its computers, **sensors**, and motor are powered by a kinetic generator—a machine that converts the energy in movement into electrical energy.

Scientists modeled their tumbleweed robots on the tumbleweed plants that roll across deserts.

Tumbleweed robots could help scientists understand how desertification happens by creating a 3D map of areas of desert. The map will show how wind and dunes interact and slowly expand a desert. The inventors of the Tumbleweed robot plan for these devices to operate on their own for years, sending information back to their operators all the time.

The rover named Zoë is equipped with a drill, cameras, and other sensors to detect life and water in the desert.

Life in the Soil?

Scientists use robots to try to understand how life survives in the driest desert on Earth. Zoë is a solar-powered robot that has sensors that can detect and map **microorganisms** and water in the soil in the Atacama Desert of northern Chile. The Atacama Desert is the driest region on Earth and possibly the most lifeless. Zoë carries a 3-foot (1 meter) drill that can collect soil samples from underground. The robot also has tools that can analyze soil samples and send this information back to scientists and researchers in their base. The Atacama Desert is the region on Earth most like Mars, so if this robot can be used to find microorganisms in the desert, it could one day be used to look for microorganisms on planet Mars, too.

MAPPING SAND AND WATER

Among the most interesting things about deserts is how dry they are and how their sand dunes shift and reform. Scientists use a variety of technology to find and measure groundwater sources and to map the movements of the dunes.

Radar

Scientists are using **radar** technology to locate and map desert groundwater. Radar detection systems attached to a helicopter can scan over 200 feet (61 meters) below the surface. By doing so, scientists can measure how much water there is and how deep these water sources are. They can also return and make new measurements to monitor any change in them. Understanding what the groundwater sources are like, and how water flows in and out of them, could be important as scientists look for ways for deserts to adapt to the effects of global warming.

Radar systems can locate and measure groundwater sources, also called aquifers, deep below the surface of the sand.

Shifting Sands

In the past, scientists tracked the movements of sand dunes across land by comparing satellite photographs. Today's cutting-edge tracking uses **lasers** that rapidly fire beams of light from satellites toward Earth. The higher the land, the quicker it takes the beam to reflect back to the satellite. The laser system uses the time it takes the beam to return to create an instant, accurate image of the shape of sandy landscapes. It can spot shifts in dunes of just 15 feet (5 meters) from 370 miles (600 kilometers) above Earth.

People in desert countries can struggle to get around and grow food when sand dunes blow over the roads, railroads, airports, and farmland.

SCIENCE PATROL SURVIVAL

Changing technology, such as satellites, radars, and drones, helps scientists cover wide areas of land and deep below desert surfaces quickly and efficiently.

Give an example of this and explain how you think this changes the way scientists work in the desert and how it could help deserts in the future.

CHAPTER 6

AMAZING DISCOVERIES

One of the most amazing discoveries scientists have made about deserts is about how they are being affected by global warming. People think that, because deserts are already hot and dry, an increase in Earth's atmosphere temperature will not affect them. However, scientists have discovered that the opposite is true.

As Earth gets warmer, deserts are at risk because Joshua trees and other plants and animals living there are already in danger of dying out.

Species Under Threat

When it comes to global warming, wildlife in the Arctic receives a lot more attention than plants in desert lands, but many plants in hot, dry climates are also under threat. The Joshua tree of the Mojave Desert, for example, is listed as "threatened" under the Endangered Species Act based on the threats posed by climate. This desert tree can grow up to 40 feet (123 meters) tall and lives an average of 150 years. Mature Joshua trees can survive on little rain but young trees need more. With drier weather, fewer trees are growing. This impacts not only the Joshua trees, but also the birds, mammals, insects, and lizards that rely on them for shelter.

Reflecting Heat

Another remarkable discovery that scientists have made is that, as desertification makes deserts spread, deserts could help cool Earth's atmosphere. This is due to the **albedo effect**. Deserts, like Arctic ice, have high albedos: their large surface areas of light-colored sand and rock reflect a large portion of the sun's heat energy that hits them. This heat escapes to space quickly through a dry atmosphere, as there are no clouds above deserts. This hot, dry air cools very quickly as it rises, and when winds blow it elsewhere, this newly cooled air helps lower the atmospheric temperature in other parts of the world.

Global warming is complicated. It threatens desert wildlife and an increase in barren desert land. However, more deserts could cool the atmosphere.

SCIENCE PATROL SURVIVAL

Scientists have discovered that the Sahara was grassland 12,000 years ago. At that time, Lake Chad was an enormous lake covering 139,000 square miles (360,000 square kilometers) of Central Africa. Today, it has shrunk to a tiny fraction of its size even 1,000 years ago.

How do you think learning about previous climate changes can help scientists understand the climate change that the world is experiencing today?

Scientists are using the discoveries they make in deserts to keep deserts and their wildlife healthy. The discoveries make a difference in other parts of the world, too.

Deserts in Distress

Scientists are finding different ways to lessen the impacts of global warming on deserts. For example, they have figured out that growing plants can anchor the soil and break the force of the wind. This prevents sand from blowing elsewhere and spreading at the edge of deserts. Watering the land is a problem in desert regions where people farm. When people use deep groundwater, this can increase salt levels in desert soils, which is bad for plants. Scientists are finding ways to use water resources more efficiently to control **salinization** and improve dry lands. They are also looking at ways to encourage more plants to grow naturally on the fringes of deserts, for example, by digging grooves in the ground that catch and trap rainfall and windblown seeds, which then germinate more easily in the damp soil.

Images like this one of the Sahara, taken from space, help scientists monitor the extent of deserts.

There are many species of darkling beetle in the Namib, and scientists are studying several types that use fog-basking as a way of getting water.

Beetle Discoveries

Scientists are also studying animals to see exactly how they survive in deserts, and how those animal adaptations can be used to help people. For example, some species of darkling beetles in the Namib Desert in Africa use their body surface to get water from dew and ocean fog. They face into the fog and stick their rear ends into the air. Microscopic bumps and grooves on the hard, front wings then help condense and channel water toward the beetle's mouth. To enable this, there are also some areas on the wings that attract water and others that repel water. In the lab, scientist are studying the exact structure of these microscopic bumps and grooves. They want to invent a mesh that people in places prone to drought could use to harvest water from the air in a similar way.

PATROLLING the FUTURE

Scientists on patrol in the desert have already learned many lessons from these arid wildernesses. If deserts of the world are to be protected and to become useful to people in the future, scientists need to continue studying and debating the science of deserts.

Working Together

There are scientists working in deserts all over the world. They do not work on their own. After they have collected and studied the data and samples they collect, they write up their results in journals or present them at conferences attended by other scientists from around the world. They share and compare results and discoveries with these other scientists. This helps them figure out if their findings are accurate and if similar problems occur in other deserts. When their results are verified, scientists can report them to the media and world governments and organizations that can use them to bring about change.

The Sahara is enormous, which means it could be used to generate solar energy across a huge area.

Working for the Future

One of the greatest challenges facing the planet is global warming. Scientists are trying to figure out if one solution could be to harvest the power of sunlight where it shines brightest: in the Sahara. Some people believe that large areas of solar panels in the Sahara could be used to supply electricity as far as away as Europe. However, others believe that technology alone cannot solve the problem of global warming. They argue that such a plan should not divert people from the long-term goal of reducing how much energy we use, and living in a more **sustainable** way. Discussions like these could impact the future of our planet.

If you could design a desert research station, what would it look like?

SCIENCE PATROL SURVIVAL

Working in remote deserts is challenging, difficult, and sometimes even dangerous. Scientists need somewhere to work productively and to live and relax comfortably. Imagine you are going to design your own research station. What will you include there?

- *Will your station consist of several buildings or only one?*
- *How many labs will you include, and what will they be used to study?*
- *How will the station be powered?*
- *What vehicles will scientists be able to use for getting around?*
- *How will the station avoid damaging the fragile desert environment?*

Glossary

adaptations the features that make a plant or animal suited to its environment or habitat

albedo effect the way the sun's energy is reflected back into space

arid very dry

atmosphere a blanket of gases around a planet

bacteria tiny living things

climate the usual pattern of weather in a particular place

condenses turns from a gas into a liquid, as water vapor cools and condenses to form liquid water

contaminated dirty or poisonous

coral reefs hard ridges in the ocean made by small animals called polyps

data facts and statistics

dehydrated describes something that has had the water removed from it

drought when an area gets so little water or rain that plants die

equator an imaginary line around the middle of the planet

erosion the process in which soil and rock are worn away by forces such as water and wind

evaporates turns from a liquid into a gas

food chains sequences of plants and animals that are linked together because each one eats or is eaten by another

friction the pushing force that slows down objects as they slide against each other

germinate to start growing

Global Positioning System (GPS) a system that uses signals from satellites in space to locate positions on Earth

groundwater water found underground in cracks and spaces in soil, sand, and rock

habitats places in nature where animals live

hypodermic needles needles used to give injections

infertile describes land that is not suitable for growing plants

lasers highly concentrated beams of light

microorganisms living things so small you need a microscope to see them

navigate to find one's way

nocturnal describes an animal that is active at night

nutrients substances that living things need to grow and be healthy

ore rock that contains useful metals or minerals

organisms living things

outback the Australian desert

particles very tiny pieces of something

phytoplankton microscopic ocean plants

precipitation any form of water that falls from the atmosphere to Earth's surface

predators animals that catch other animals for food

radar a way of finding the position of an object by bouncing a radio wave off it and analyzing the reflected wave

salinization the process by which soil becomes salty

samples representative parts or single items from a larger whole or group

satellite an electronic device high in space that moves around Earth

semidesert an area that is almost desert but that gets a little more rain than a true desert

sensors devices that detect and measure something, such as the amount of gases in the air

solar power electricity made from sunlight

specimens individual animals, plants, or minerals used as examples of their type for scientific study

sustainable describes a way of using something without completely using up or destroying it

tropics the regions of Earth on either side of the equator

ultraviolet (UV) invisible beams of light within sunlight that can damage skin

venom a poison made by some animals for defense or to stun or kill prey

wind turbines machines that capture the wind's energy to make electricity

For More Information

Books

Clarek, Ginjer L. *What's Up in the Gobi Desert?* New York, NY: Grosset & Dunlap, 2016.

Cohen, Marina. *Deserts Inside Out* (Ecosystems Inside and Out). St. Catherines, ON: Crabtree Publishing Company, 2014.

Spilsbury, Richard, and Louise Spilsbury. *At Home in the Desert* (A Home in the Biome). New York, NY: PowerKids Press, 2016.

Websites

Read more about deserts at:
www.environment.nationalgeographic.com/environment/habitats/desert-profile

Discover more about deserts and why the Arctic and Antarctica are known as cold deserts at:
www.kids.nceas.ucsb.edu/biomes/desert.html

Learn more about the Sonoran Desert at:
www.desertmuseum.org/kids/oz

There is more information about deserts at:
www.cotf.edu/ete/modules/msese/earthsysflr/desert.html

Publisher's note to educators and parents: Our editors have carefully reviewed these websites to ensure that they are suitable for students. Many websites change frequently, however, and we cannot guarantee that a site's future contents will continue to meet our high standards of quality and educational value. Be advised that students should be closely supervised whenever they access the Internet.

index

adaptations 10, 11, 43
Africa 5, 16, 41, 43
albedo effect 41
Altyn-Emel National Park 7
Amazon rainforest 17
animals 4, 8, 10, 11, 12, 13, 15, 18, 21, 31, 32, 33, 40, 43
Arabian Desert 14
Arizona 5
Asia 16
Atacama Desert 5, 37
Australia 5, 16

bacteria 17, 20, 25

California 22
camels 27, 33
camera traps 32
Chile 5, 37
climate 6, 21, 40, 41
clothes 28
cloud seeding 35
clouds 13, 29, 30, 35, 41
coastal deserts 5, 7
coral reefs 17

darkling beetle 43
data 6, 18, 30, 36, 44
Desert Research and Technology Studies (RATS) 24, 25
Desert Studies Center (DSC) 22, 23
desert tortoises 11, 15, 32, 33
desertification 12–13, 37, 41
drought 10, 12, 13, 43
dust 16–17, 19, 29, 30

equipment 19, 23, 26, 28, 30
evaporative cooling 21

fennec fox 11
flic-flac spider 11
fog 5, 7, 43
food 11, 13, 31, 36, 39
food chains 15, 17

gila monsters 9
Global Positioning System (GPS) 26, 33
global warming 13, 17, 38, 40, 41, 42, 45
Gobi 5
groundwater 14, 20, 38, 42

heatstroke 6
heliostats 34

inland deserts 5

Joshua trees 40

Kalahari 5
Kazakhstan 7

labs 6, 18–19, 20, 21, 22–23, 24, 25, 33, 43, 45
Lake Chad 41
Las Vegas 34
lasers 39
LOCAD 25

Mars 24, 25, 37
minerals 14, 17, 20, 22
mining 14, 22
Mojave Desert 22, 40
Morocco 11

Namib Desert 43
navigation 26
Nevada 34

oases 4, 13, 22, 23
overgrazing 12

photovoltaic panels 20, 34
phytoplankton 17
PI-SWERL 19
plants 4, 8, 10, 11, 12, 13, 14, 15, 17, 18, 23, 27, 31, 34, 36, 40, 42

radar 38, 39
rain 4, 5, 6, 7, 10, 12, 13, 17, 34–35, 40, 42
rain shadow desert 5
rattlesnakes 9
red brome grass 15
roadrunner 11
robots 35, 36–37

Sahara 5, 6, 17, 41, 42, 44, 45
salinization 42
salt 29, 34, 35, 42
samples 6, 23, 30, 37, 44
sand 4, 5, 7, 8, 9, 19, 26, 27, 28, 29, 32, 35, 38–39, 41, 42
Saudi Arabia 14
scorpions 8, 11, 29
semidesert 12
Sierra Nevada mountains 5
smartphone software 33
solar power 20, 34
Sonoran Desert 10
species recognition 32
springs 20, 22
stings 8, 29
subtropical deserts 5
sun 8, 11, 20, 21, 28, 29, 30, 34, 35, 41

Tanami Desert 5
temperatures 6, 13, 30, 40, 41
tents 30
tourism 14, 15

vehicles 15, 18, 24, 26, 27, 30, 45
venom 8, 9, 29

water 4, 7, 9, 10, 11, 12, 13, 14, 15, 20, 23, 31, 34, 35, 36, 37, 38, 42, 43
Wildland Fire Science Center 18
wind 4, 5, 7, 12, 15, 16, 17, 19, 20, 26, 29, 30, 36, 37, 41, 42